D0167279

The bright red horse—and the blue—
Poems

Katy Lederer

a t e l o s

39

ISBN: 978-1891190-39-1

First edition, first printing

Ŧ Atelos

A Project of Hip's Road
Editors: Lyn Hejinian & Travis Ortiz
Text and Cover Design and Typesetting: Derek Fenner
Cover Image: Franz Marc, *Stables* (1913); reproduced with permission
of the Guggenheim Museum, New York City.

Contents

Numbers

The bright red horse—and the blue—
Slaughter one another—
And the twenty-four oxen
A third of the trees
And a third of the ships
In their tails—
Like moths

And the one in your mouth—
Is put on
With the right hand—
So that no one can
Buy or sell—
Having come
A distance
Of about two
Miles

And every living thing
Was dead—
The women
And the men
Put on a mouth

This calls to mind
The seven heads
And the ten names—
The four living creatures
Fell down—
And outside—
The dogs—
To the south and to the north—

The wall is built of
Jasper

And its length and height are equal—
And the east three gates—
The ones
Who say—
The filthy still be
Filthy and the

Outside the dogs—so
Those who
Have not—
I will
Give them
A mouth—
I am throwing on
A mouth

A Person

We begin with
A thought—
With a doctrine—
Of the sympathy
Of thought—

The love-region becomes
This—that I have—
Exactly
The world of—
Vision—
Into this—
The picture of—
The idea of—
The drama—

We may enter it
Directly—
We may work it out
Our own way—

As in—say
More—
Or your
Urge—
To help you with—
A thought

The lines of—certain words of—
And I know this—
We begin—with—

With a person—
So—developed—
We begin with—
With—a person

Numbers

The more prominent
Themes—
In the form of
A woman—
Not ceasing—
Through eating—
The greater
Delight—
In the lesser—
And the greater—
Of the members—
Of his body—
Were this

And made like itself—
It is turned
Toward—the higher—
And made in itself—
In the image of
The lesser—
That is—
In his eyes—that
Turn toward
The figure—
To turn toward
The lesser one—
Once and
For all

The eyes—to be sure—
Are intended

To conjure—
A posited nipple—
A southern-faced
Pole—

For the men and
The women—
The eyes—
Somewhat girlish—

The eyes—
On the face
Of the Christ—
And seen too: the huge

Fishing Mary—
The huge and big-breasted
Mary and Clare and Lidwina
Of Schiedam—

Impasse

What she said—
It was important—
It came up throughout
The person—
At the bottoms of
Her feet and then—
The bottom of
Her heart

The heart it has
A trap-door—
With the heart—
The destination—
At the other end—
Another heart—

As it creeps
And it is in—
And its feet must leave
Its heart—
And it entered through
The bottom-of-the-feet—
And it reached
Its destination—

It came cooing like
A pigeon—
With the feathers used
For traction—
Walking through—
The person's body—
On the two small tips of its wings—

As in stilts—
Or as on—
Crutches—
And the joints became
Like rungs—
On the body like
A ladder—

Through the person came—
Emotion—
It swept briskly through
The person

Numbers

A person
Was stated—
A person—
I think so—
The thin ones—
I think it—
It—chosen
Above all—

A sort of—
The low wall—
A thousand—
A hundred—
Who wrote it—
To choose it—
The born by
The have it

I kept—at
The low walls—
The chosen—one—
Chosen
To keep—
Each one—
Thin ones—
And—fat ones—
And have her—
Accept her—
And flatter—
It out—

Or the—palest—
The pressure
Of waiting—
The years—
Two or more—

To some—
It is many—
To some
It is
Two years

Famish and Gorge

I am the voice
That stands low on
The perch of—
Surmises

Sometimes—
Me—
All the time—
Never—
For always—
But maybe—
The juster
Amount

The revels are
At last
Begun—

If I shoot out this
Bullet
To begin them

It is this—
That I
Myself—
Will bloat—

The harvest before—
All the leaves
Will turn over—

So feed us—
It's good—
But I cannot
Digest it—and
If it is not
Too much—pain
To have—known it—

The last place we
Couldn't have gone
Would be up

Unburthened

To listen—
Confess—
As I—
As I—
I do not—

I gain by—
And it is—
This charity in them

What profit—
I gain by—
My past—this—
I have declared

For at least—
What I speak—
It is true

And how does it—
Profit—
Their hearts—
In this way—
For you—

Tell them—you—
This way—you—
That way—(I cannot)

I cannot—
I cannot—
I am so—
I cannot

Grievous Oppressing

What is the matter—
When I heard
They said to—
They told him
These words—
"We will give ourselves up"

They reported the matter—
The people—
They told him—
So all of the people
"We'll serve you—
(We've listened)"

The one—who will
Lead you—
The one who is
Old—
He will come
In the morning—
The next day
And so forth—

The people
Reported—
"There's no one
To save us"
"There's—
No one—to
Save us"
"We'll give ourselves—
Up to you"

Pulling It Off

He touched her—
The table came off

She took this—
He did—

It came off—and
The table—

Came off
He put his hands

Out—
Imagine it

Off—it came
Off

Overthrow the Event

He creates the event—
I am one of those—
The impression by me—

Usurping the feelings of others—
Creating the event—

Sick toward whom—
Creates the event—
Anguish to him—

Some are
Overthrown by it—

He visits—
Escapes it—

So say now the
Said it—

Numbers

For I have—
And I have
My reach in this
Thing—

And I am some—
Two men—
That he—but he
Did not—

Why one—so that
I am—

And one had some—
I am—

We had some—
If one some—

Is that—if
Two did—

But all try—
Their something:

One did—he
Did want to—

The other did not

Crime Begins These Laws

He is not
My strong point—
You think

We will go far—
It must have been
Really true—
You think

Following these
Laws

The whole point
Being—
For a moment—
What's the point?

Then he stole it—
Thinking

Crime requires—
Going away—
Narrowly escaping—
The strong
Hold

Escape—
You think—
Is a hazard—

In order to steal—
You think—
One must respond

To Perform and to Reveal

The guises—
Of persons—he
Came to her—

Performance
Between them—impulses—

The artifice
Between them—
In the guise of—
Artifice—

Sun in the sky—rain—
Impulses
Stilled—

To perform—turning
Back to the hand—

The guises of
Stilled—
Repetitions—

Comparative, level—
The morning—
Between them—

Plentiful There

The emotions
But are—
The antagonists—

Evening fell—and
Inflamed him—

Undid then—
Consumed him

Respecting the spring—
With them
Taking a pitcher—

The sentinels—
Frenzied
With thirst—

According to the Appetites

Let birds—let fly—
That it was good—
There was a night
And then a day—
And every living
Creature moved—
Was good

The light was good—
The air—the man—
The man became
A living thing—
And there he put
The man
Who formed
The earth—
No rain, no no

When you touch—
Delight—
You will not
Die

The door—
The door—
Is hard to bear—

I shall be hidden—
Nothing sweet—
Your days—
Your face—
And now you might—

And at the east—
Which he—
Was taken—
Turned away—
And heard
The voice:

I am—open—
I am—out—
The firstlings—and—
The seedlings

I Kind Of (a Voice)

I kind of—
Or how at—
Or kind of a flower—
Was up there—
A clearing—
Before—
Of a clearing—

You speak—
If I talk—
I have something—
To then to—

I've fallen on—
Saw him—

I find myself
Calling him:
"Don't try
To follow me"—

And he was just
Up—

You must never—
Talk and talk—

But his voice—
It is
"Touch him"

Ode

I wait
For its name—and—
Look—
How the tree
Comes to—
Sing to it—
Wait—
Then harass it

I make myself
Like this—
And ask for—
The tree—
Is the weight of—
The tree—
And awaiting my—
Certainly—
Musical form—
It will quiver—and
As it were—
Naked

And this—
The idea of
The tree—

Yes to thee—
My one beech—yes—
My happy done
Birch tree—
You are so—

I want it—
I come—
Hang my belt from the—
Move me—the
All me—

The sun comes—
And midday—is
Felt about
Your tufted shade

You hear
That I hear—
The barest of leaves—
And

The beech tree—
The birch tree—
The tree—
It will have me

Desire

And then he kept—
On top
Of the roof—
An undesirable—
Sometimes cold—

Later in the room—
In her palm—
Last in
The palm of
Desire

On the bottom stair—
Unwinding—
Coming into
The warm
Water—

And then he kept
Ringing—
Mentioning bells—
The life
Inside—

He could answer—in
The hallway—
His palm was put
Out—
He put his hand
Out—for her

It was how he
Used to be—

He ran the water—
Drew himself in—

Because of nature—
He was there

Before the Leaves

Beneath these
Trees—
We promised—magnificent
Trees—

Assembled
To collect
The seeds—
The boughs—stripped—

The seeds—
As in—
Evidence—
Waiting

As a Matter of Course

Distress—upon
The beach—
Intense—for salt—for
Stalking waves

Obtained a passage
From
The beach—
A passage—talk—
A passage—much—
Our distress—and

Especially—
Broadly
Defined—as
Distress—was

The visiting ship—which
Would ship out—
Enough—

But of late—we
Remained—
There—a week—the long boat
Is then ready—
To depart

Repeated Omission

There was no—
Probability—it—
Hardly possible—

All of his perilous—
Thoroughly
Sensible—
No possibility—

Otherwise capable—
Otherwise
Irresolute—
His perception
Which had—for it

Hardly—his
Intoxication—
Would have him
Beneath—
All the—
Evident daybreak

Inconsequential—the—
Hardly
Improbable—
Turn of events—

In the interim—probable—
Inconsequential and—
Frequently—
Possible—

Otherwise—
No—
It—is—
Possible—
Only—

That merely—
That only—
The sensible—
Possible—

Your Cities and You

Your cities and you—
Who are mountains—
Shall
Return—

In the days of—
But who will—
There shall be—
Just as in—
The orchard
Shall ripen—
Shall
Eat—
Die of
Hunger—
Shall die of—
Shall hunger—
And naught—but
To eat

Those—open—
Shall—open—
Your beautiful face—

When you
Were will—
And—shall will—

And I ought to—
You shall—

And all your—
Shall—
Who
Shall you—
You shall—
And I—we

Shall be
In the cities—
Which will be
The country—

The mountains—shall—
You
And your cities—
And you

Turn, Oh You Turn

Straining—
Stolen by fauns

It is August—
Oh no

It's September
Already

No Means

Forced—to allow—
He had—ever—
Been seen
He was
No means—by no means
Was—
Through—one direction
When
Through—two or three of them—

Forced—to allow—
He was—
Forced to—allow them—
To—
Hear—not to—
Hear—

Her by—
No means—
Some trouble—

To hear—him
No means
To be—had

To Perfect an Imitation of Myself

I will not venture—
To venture—in spite of
Myself—
To venture—in spite of
My general
Defect—

Identical—
Did he—
Did he—play—
His part?

Consolation—
Alone—all
Alone—me—
Myself

Did he play me—
Myself—
Did he—did he—
Without me?

Without me—
In fact—that he
Played me—
Myself

I will not—
Did he—
I will
Not not—

Did he
Play me—
Not
Play me—myself—

Did he
Play—me—myself?

I Want the Damages

I want the damages—
Good—get me
Down—when
I had a—
I had a—
Respectable
Moment

Oh—my—
Strict integrity—
My strict economy—
Prodigal heir of
The usual businesslike—
Old—operations

Oh—please—
Contemplation

This done—we wait—
Waiting

And yet—
There were rascally—we
Corporations

Avoid a connection
We will—that we
Can can—
Avoid—
Good old
Sober and
Rigorous business

Refrain

You have nothing
To give—
But you've got to—
The pocket

You count
At the gate—
You have
Nothing—
To give—

The lucrative contract—
The lucrative contract—

The pocket—
You've got to—
You've nothing—
To give

An Angel Marks a Grave

A wing interferes with
The tree—
Interferes with—the
Tree—interferes
With the wing—
Interferes—with
The tree—
The tree then—
With me—

Interfering—the
Tree—interfering with me

And the wing interferes with
The tree—
Interfering with
Me—and
The tree—interfering
With me

Interfering with
Me—and
The tree—
Thus the wing—
Interfering with
Me—and
The tree—and
With me—and
The tree—a
Stone wing—
Interfering with
Me—and

The wing—the
Stone wing—
Interfering with
Me—and

The tree—and
The tree—thus
With me

Surnamed the Hater

For what we had—
We shunned—
A wicked man—

And with so little
Contact—
We did not
Believe him—

The thing in
Itself was a—
Green bright dark bitter

And I have been
Stripped upon
Entry—we are never on
Expedition—at all—
Nor is this an
Unraveling passage—

I think—
At the table
We are—
Far too philosophical

Bacchante

I've come to
Free you—
In that—
Only then—
Before—
You had
Someone

When the moment
Comes
For him
To go—
You know—
This is a place—
You really don't
Know—
Worse off—
You really—
Suppose
That you do

I'm not sure
What
I ought
To do

They don't know
How
To laugh

Do you mean—
Nothing good?
You know—
Nothing
You're troubled—
And—one day is
Done—which
You do not know—

And yet—
You really
Suppose that
You do

Numbers

Then he went away—
The owner of this
House—so he—

The one who had received the one—

The one who had—
Received—the
Two—

And those—who have—
Will take
Away—

I know—
You will have what is yours

Afterword

In 1995, Lyn Hejinian and Travis Ortiz asked me for a book. They were starting a new press, Atelos, which they described as a home for books that challenged conventional definitions of poetry. I was flattered, but abashed. I was twenty-two years old, and I didn't yet feel ready to be that public with my work. There was, first of all, the matter of my coterie, which consisted of many brilliant young poets who were achieving incredible things in the conceptual or New Narrative modes, but who mainly looked askance (though always with the utmost affection) at my lyric sensibility. Second, and more immediately, I simply didn't have a book, and I found it difficult to imagine I would write one.

It was at this same time I was writing this book. Starting in the spring of '95, my last semester at Berkeley, where I had worked closely with Lyn, and running through the fall of '96, which was my first semester at the Writers' Workshop in Iowa, I wrote a series of un-lineated lyric poems punctuated only by dashes. The first in the series was a poem called "West" that I would do nothing with because it was not good. "Impasse," which is included here, came next. (All told, I composed fifty-six poems in this form; thirty-one are included here.) I was at the time just beginning to fall in love. The person was ostensibly available, but was in fact unavailable to me, and I pursued him with the self-destructive vigor of a person who has never had a broken heart. All through that year, which I spent for the most part in Las Vegas and San Francisco, I wrote my un-lineated, "dash" poems. I did not think of myself as writing a series or as working on a project. Often, I would open a book I was reading at the time, skim the pages for words of interest or attraction, make what I thought of as music (the content was secondary). The poems were an intellectual Rorschach, and their form was a generative template for emotions that ran the gamut from ravishment to sympathy to dread. But yet I told Lyn I did not have a book, I had nothing (and in some sense this was true—I had desire and then abjection, and the poems seemed the dead remains).

so interesting

The poems were also in block-form with no enjambment or breaks, uninviting and impossible to scan. I see now I was seeking protection—formal and emotional—from both the other poets and the person I had fallen for. (It is embarrassing to admit this now, this urge to hide in form, but I believe it is a reality for many poets.) Some friends from my old coterie started a chapbook press, and they asked me for poems. I gave them several pieces from the series, but they appeared as intimidating blocks, and, however interesting to look at, were very difficult to read. The students at Iowa didn't know what to make of them. I believe some peers might have suggested that I open them up, but, whatever the feedback, I left the poems as they were, hard and un-scalable walls.

Three years ago, after having my children, I felt a strong urge to organize my life. The poems from my twenties had been transferred from one computer to another, placed willy-nilly in documents and emails, and many had become impossible to access. I decided it was time to gather everything together in one place, and, in the process, I rediscovered the poems here. Over the course of several days I worked to revise them. I could finally see them for what they were, which were beseeching lyric prayers: fierce, sad, quizzical, angry, tender, and bereft, and I wanted to release them from their blocks into an open form. I was no longer the frustrated young woman who composed these complex poems, and I felt for her, her pain and rage. I also admired her, the powerful muscularity of her music and the sophisticated raiment of her dashes, which, to me, represent so many things: parries and thrusts, bars (as in a prison), invitations, suffocations, breaths, and lashes of the heart.

When I first showed the series to Lyn—twenty years after she and Travis had asked for a book; twenty years after I had composed it—she commented that the poems read as "in the beginnings of emotion." This was a beautiful characterization, generous, sunny, and loving. But I believe that in fact the series exists at the end—the end of pure emotion, of youthful innocence and love. They are the record of a heart being broken. I remember then, when I wrote the poems here, not comprehending the transformation that was happening to me, unaware that I would never be the same. And I recall a few years later, once the passion had abated, understanding, finally, that ubiquitous expression: "a broken heart"; like a horse that has been broken. After that first heartbreak, one is, in some sense, mastered—by the knowledge of and avoidance of pain, and by the empathy for all the other people in this world who have been broken.

Acknowledgments

I want to thank the editors of the following journals in which some of these poems appeared (most in different forms, and many with different titles):

Gare du Nord: "According to the Appetites"; "To Perfect an Imitation of Myself"
The Harvard Review: "Impasse"
The Iowa Journal of Cultural Studies: "Ode"
Lana Turner: "Plentiful There"; "Surnamed the Hater"
Mike and Dale's Younger Poets: "Numbers ('The more prominent')"
Nat. Brut: "Numbers ('For I have—')"; "Repeated Omission"; "Pulling It Off"
Prosodia: "Numbers ('The bright red horse—and the blue—')"

Gratitude to the following intellectual and poetic inspirations and sources: *The Bible* (The New Revised Standard Version. Bruce Metzger and Roland Murphy, eds., New York: Oxford University Press), Poe, Valéry, H.D., Pavese, Caroline Walker Bynum, Steven Goldsmith, and Stefania Pandolfo.

Grateful acknowledgment is made to Alex Cory, Pamela Lu, and everyone else at Idiom, who published a chapbook titled *Faith* that included many of these poems; and to David Lehman for selecting "According to the Appetites" (in a different form) for inclusion in *Great American Prose Poems: from Poe to the Present* (Scribner's). "According to the Appetites" and "Ode" were included in different forms in my first book, *Winter Sex* (Verse Press). Thanks to Lyn Hejinian, Jorie Graham, and Gillian Conoley for working with me as I was composing these poems; and thanks to Mark Bibbins, Idra Novey, Lucy Ives, Jennifer Firestone, and Prageeta Sharma for reading versions of the poems as I revisited their forms. Thanks also to Derek Fenner and Victoria Kornick for their patience and discernment.

Katy Lederer is the author of the poetry collections *Winter Sex* (Verse/Wave) and *The Heaven-Sent Leaf* (BOA Editions), as well as of the memoir *Poker Face: A Girlhood Among Gamblers* (Crown). From 1997 to 2007 she edited *Explosive Magazine*, a mimeo poetry journal featuring art work and design by David Larsen and Dave Morice. From 2005 to 2014, she served as a Poetry Editor for *Fence Magazine*.

The bright red horse—and the blue—
was printed in an edition of 500 copies
at Thomson-Shore, Inc.
Text and cover design and typesetting by Derek Fenner
using the old-style serif typeface Garamond.

Atelos was founded in 1995 as a project of Hips Road and is devoted to publishing, under the sign of poetry, writing that challenges conventional, limiting definitions of poetry. All the works published as part of the Atelos project are commissioned specifically for it, and each is involved in some way with crossing traditional genre boundaries, including, for example, those that would separate theory from practice, poetry from prose, essay from drama, the visual image from the verbal, the literary from the non-literary, and so forth. The Atelos project when complete will consist of 50 volumes.

The project directors and editors are Lyn Hejinian and Travis Ortiz. The director for design, cover production, and text production is Derek Fenner.

Atelos (current volumes):
1. The Literal World, by Jean Day
2. Bad History, by Barrett Watten
3. True, by Rae Armantrout
4. Pamela: A Novel, by Pamela Lu
5. Cable Factory 20, by Lytle Shaw
6. R-hu, by Leslie Scalapino
7. Verisimilitude, by Hung Q. Tu
8. Alien Tatters, by Clark Coolidge
9. Forthcoming, by Jalal Toufic
10. Gardener of Stars, by Carla Harryman
11. lighthouse, by M. Mara-Ann
12. Some Vague Wife, by Kathy Lou Schultz
13. The Crave, by Kit Robinson
14. Fashionable Noise, by Brian Kim Stefans
15. Platform, by Rodrigo Toscano
16. Tis of Thee, by Fanny Howe
17 Poetical Dictionary, by Lohren Green
18. BlipSoak01, by Tan Lin
19. The Up and Up, by Ted Greenwald
20. Noh Business, by Murray Edmond

Distributed by:

Small Press Distribution
1341 Seventh Street
Berkeley, California
    94710-1403

Atelos
P O Box 5814
Berkeley, California
    94705-0814

to order from SPD call 510-524-1668 or toll-free 800-869-7553
fax orders to: 510-524-0852
order via e-mail at: orders@spdbooks.org
order online from: www.spdbooks.org